You, Me, and Your Retirement Years

Let's Flamingle

by

SANDRA O'FARRELL

To order additional copies of this book, contact:
Xlibris
844-714-8691
www.Xlibris.com
Orders@Xlibris.com

ISBN: Softcover   979-8-3694-3662-2
        EBook   979-8-3694-3663-9

Print information available on the last page

Rev. date: 12/11/2024

Donald O'Farrell
(Retired)

I dedicate this book to him.

TO; ALL OF MY NEW READERS. THIS IS A WORK THAT I HAVE LONG THOUGHT ABOUT DOING. IT IS TRULY A BOOK FOR ANYONE Contemplating AND CONSIDERING RETIREMENT. When first I did retire I did not like the loneliness and the boredom that retirement brought to my older life so three months later I starting looking for work once again with my resume in my hand. I was lucky and became a working women once again. My book is dedicated to everyone who will retire in the next five to 15 years.

Sandra O'Farrell
80 yrs. old
Retired at 62 yrs.

Sandra O'Farrell
Navarre, Florida

Poet, Writer
Swim Instructor
(now retired)

I Sandra O'Farrell, have a wonderful pass time, teaching children to swim. I have been so blessed doing this in my retirement years!

THIS IS A BOOK FOR PERSONS WHO ARE BORED TO PIECES AFTER THEY DO RETIRE AND ARE NOW LOOKING HARD FOR THEIR RETIREMENT TO BE FUN AND EXCITING TOO. ON THIS FIRST PAGE I WILL GIVE SUGGESTIONS AS TO SOME OF THE THINGS I FOUND TO GIVE MY LIFE MEANING AFTER I RETIRED. FIRST, YOU MUST REMEMBER THAT YOU HAVE WAITED YOUR WHOLE LIFE TO GET TO THE POINT THAT YOU DO NOT HALF TO GET UP EARLY EVERY SINGLE DAY AND RUSH TO GET READY FOR WORK EACH AND EVERY DAY NOW. YOU, DO NOT HAVE TO FIGHT TRAFFIC IN THE MORNINGS ARE TRY TO EAT SOME OF YOUR BREAKFAST RUSHING OUT OF THE DOOR, MORNINGS WHEN YOU ARE RUNNING LATE. YOUR SPOUSE IF YOU DO HAVE ONE MUST BE NEAR RETIREMENT YEARS WITH YOU SO SHE NO LONGER HAS TO LOOK PERFECT AS SHE CAN, TO BE READY TO LEAVE WITH YOU SOME MORNINGS, SHE CAN NOW RELAX AND DRINK ALL OF THE COFFEE THAT SHE WANTS TO WITHOUT FEELING GUILTY, JUST SITTING BACK RELAXING AND READING HER PAPER OR HER NOTES. SOME DAYS IT WILL SEEM STRANGE THAT YOU ARE NOT RUSHING AT ALL AN NOT GOING INTO A JOB THAT YOU HAD FOR SO LONG OF A TIME.

THIS IS A REAL EVENT THAT ACTUALLY DID HAPPEN AND WAS TOTALLY AND COMPLETELY ENJOYED BY ALL OF US IN OUR FAMILY WHO DID TAKE THE TIME AND THE EFFORT TO CHANGE OUR LIVES AS WE GOT OLDER. GOING TO ORLANDO, FLORIDA TO TRY AND SUCQURE A JOB AT DISNEY WORLD AND PRAY THAT SOMEONE OVER THERE WOULD EITHER HIRE MY HUSBAND DON, TO DO MAINTENANCE WORK AT DISNEY OR HIRE MYSELF TO WRITE OR DRAW OR SING FOR THEM AS I DO WRITE POETRY AND SHORT STORIES AN I DO SING. A FACT IS THAT ON OUR WAY HOME FROM THERE WE RAN INTO A BACK ROADS OF A VERY SMALL TOWN OUT IN NO WHERE LAND BECAUSE WE WERE LOST AND OFF THE MAIN ROADS. IT SEEMED TO BE A NICE PLACE WHERE WE RAN INTO A LARGE TWO STORY HOUSE WHICH SEEMED TO BE EMPTY AT THE TIME.

IT WAS NOT THAT I WAS SICK OR JUST GOT A HUNCH ABOUT ANYONE THING THERE BUT DECIDED TO LEAVE THE OWNER OF THIS BEAUTIFUL HOME A LETTER TO SAY TO THEM WE WOULD JUST LOVE TO RENT THIS HOME FROM THEM. WE DID LEAVE OUR TELEPHONE NUMBER

AND ASKED THAT THEY MIGHT WHENEVER THEY COULD LET US KNOW WHAT THEY THOUGHT OF THIS NEW IDEA, TO RENT THEIR HOME TO US. I DID RECEIVE A LOVELY CALL AND THE LADY SAID, SHE WOULD RENT HER SON'S HOME TO US. WE FINALLY DECIDED ON A PRICE SO WE STARTED TO MOVE TO THIS AREA. IT TOOK A LOT OUT OF US BECAUSE WE WERE SENIORS AND MOVING WAS VERY HARD ON US. OUR HOUSE BACK HOME WE WOULD THEN PUT UP ON THE MARKET FOR SALE.

AFTER WE MOVED I WOULD GO OUT TO FISH IN OUR NEW BACK YARD AND CATCH THE FISH OF THE DAY WHICH WAS BITTING THAT DAY, MOSTLY LARGE CAT FISH AND ALL OF US IN OUR NEW HOME ON THE BAY LOVED TO CRAB SO WE WOULD PUT OUT CRAB TRAPS AT CERTAIN TIMES AND GET CRABS TO BOIL THAT NIGHT. WHAT A WONDERFUL TIME WE ALL HAD THERE. MORNINGS WE WOULD JUST DRIVE FIVE MILES DOWN THE ROAD TO THE GORGEOUS BEACHES AND TAKE OUT THE CHILDREN TO SWIMM. WE LOVED TO PICNIC AND TO GO TO LITTLE SHOPS AND TO JUST LOOK AROUND FOR SEA SHELLS ON SALE. (SOME OF THESE BEACHES ARE NOW STILL THE SAME LOVELY

WHITE SANDS). TRY GRAYTON BEACH. ALSO THERE IS THE TOWN OF MEXICO BEACH, AND PANAMA CITY BEACHES, DAYTONIA BEACH, MARCO ISLAND, NAVARRE BEACH, PENSACOLA BEACH, AND SANTA ROSA BEACHES. GRAYTON BEACH IS ONE OF THE FAVORITES AND NOT SO CROWDED. DESTIN, FLORIDA IS ALSO A FAVORITE.

BACK TO OUR NEW HOME. IN THE EVENING WE ALL WOULD TAKE THE TIME TO WALK ALL AROUND THE NEIGHBORHOOD AND OUR LITTLE BLACK CAT WOULD COME OUT WITH OUR DOG NAMED SHOTTSIE AND WALK RIGHT BEHIND US, HAVING THE TIME OF THERE LIVES. ON SAT. I WOULD TAKE OUT ALL OF OUR BIKES SO WE COULD GO BIKE RIDING WHICH IS ALSO A GOOD THING FOR RETIRED PERSONS WHO LOVE THE RIDE AND THE FRESH AIR. THIS IS IF, YOU ARE STILL WELL ENOUGH TO GET UP ON A BIKE AND PEDDLE THE BICYCLE. REMEMBER, MEMORIES ARE MADE OF SUCH TIMES AS THIS.

Lazy days

This is a chapter to just let you all know that the time you spend doing nothing at all would be an excellent time to start off a project in the hobby of wood working. this is a fun and an active thing to do during your spare time hours of your day. one time we had a neighbor who got so good at this that he started to sell all of his wood working projects at a market near his house and had a very good income from all of his efforts. first, get yourself a sturdy and well made small wood saw that cuts out patterns on wood. then find a nice table to do your wood working on. last remember, when your projects are nearly through with, you will want to paint them so buy a large set of wood paints at a hobbie shop nearest to your house. All of the bellow projects i myself have seen you they looked just great when finished.

1. *Wooden picture frames to put your family pictures in.*
2. *Magazine racks, then varnish them or paint them with your favorite color to match your decore.*
3. *HOBBY HORSES OR UNICORNS.*
4. *BIRD HOUSES.*
5. *small chests to hold your jewelry or keys.*
6. *Wooden toilet paper holders to place on your bathroom floors. Also wooden boxes to put your knitting or art work in.*

Chapter 5

fishing for: Woodworking Supplies

THERE ARE SO MANY GREAT HOBBIES TO CHOOSE FROM AND ONE OF THESE HOBBIES IS (WOODWORKING.) IT IS SO REWARDING TO PICK THIS UP AND START IT.

all OF THE SUPPLIES YOU WILL NEED IS AS FOLLOWS; *you need a table for the start of you woodworking projects.* TRY AN OLDER ONE SO IT CAN BE DAMAGED AND YOU WILL NOT LOOSE ANY MONEY ON SUCH A TABLE. NOW, THE NEXT THING YOU NEED TO BUY IS A SAW TO CUT OUT SMALL PIECES OF WOOD. THIS IS NOT TOO EXPENSIVE TO BUY. THE NEXT IS A SET OF PAINTS TO PAINT YOUR WOOD WORKING PROJECTS. ALL OF YOUR SUPPLIES CAN BE KEPT IN A LARGE EMPTY COFFEE CAN. ALL OF THE NICEST AND WELL LOVED PROJECTS CAN BE PLANNED AHEAD OF TIME. THESE ARE JUST A FEW OF THEM: TRY CUTTING OUT A HOBBY HORSE OR A

Sandra & Donald O'Farrell
"PIRATE PARTY"

Dances & Balls

their retirement years.

This is a fun and rewarding hobby and will not cost you too much to start this project off. Anyway, lots of people like to paint because it is so relaxing.

In most communities around the country, even in small towns now are good and informative libraries. If you can still drive, this would be a relaxing and nice outing to go to, your local libraries, to check out some books you might like to read. If you like to be around other people such as yourself, then stay in the library and read some of the books which you chose there. Most libraries have large tables you can sit and read at. They do not limit your reading time.

If you enjoy fishing you can invest in some really nice rods and reels and pick up a nice map to see just which states have some really nice lakes or rivers to fish in. One small town is Grand Isle, Louisiana. The family I am in, used to go over there to fish

(Chapter 4)

THESE: NEXT PAGES WILL GIVE EVERYONE OF MY READERS A CHANCH TO GET UP OUT OF YOUR EASY CHAIR OR SOFA AND START TAKING PART IN REAL LIFE FUNCTIONS AND OUTINGS. THIS PART OF THIS BOOK GIVES A PERSON WHO NOW HAS A VERY BORING LIFE. THE TRICK TO MOST OF THIS IS SO EASY. IF YOU DO NOT ALREADY HAVE AN OUTSIDE ACTIVITY OF SOME KIND, BY ALL MEANS START THINKING ABOUT WHAT YOU DO LIKE TO DO AND NO MATTER WHAT YOUR AGE NOW, GO FOR IT IN YOUR FUTURE.

ALL OF US ARE SOME OF US LIKE TO DANCE AND BE AROUND PEOPLE OUR OWN AGE TO TALK TO

WE MUST KNOW SOME ONE WHO IS ALREADY IN A CLUB OR A CARD PARTY CLOSE AROUND OUR TOWN. THE PEOPLE WHO PLAY CARD GAMES, USUALLY TAKE IN NEW MEMBERS AT LEAST ONCE OR TWICE A YEAR SO IF YOU CAN NOT GET INTO THIS GROUP, TRY PUTTING YOUR NAME ON A WAITING LIST SO THAT THEY WILL CALL YOU IN THE FUTURE, TO JOIN THEM. Next, so many clubs are invitation only by other club members. If you are lucky enough to be asked to join them, by all means please do this. These clubs have dances, bus trips for everyone of their members, balls, picnics, luncheons, Christmas parties also. The fun of all of this is it keeps you interested in going out and getting all dressed up. One club I know about, even has a big pirate party once a year now. lots of fun there.

Let us introduce you to the American South and show you all the great sights and port cities as we cruise the legendary Mississippi River between New Orleans to Memphis. A new chapter awaits as we cruise around each river bend.

Chapter 5

Buy Next:
A woodworking saw!

set and a little FIND A FEW SUGGESTIONS AS saw to FIND A FEW SUGGESTIONS AS cut out your wood working projects. After the project you pick, like maybe some wooden picture frames or maybe a wooden hobby horse of some kind or a magazine container to place next to your favorite easy chair, keep in mind these items are very useful for yourself or for gifts in the future. Next, you will probably want to purchase a paint set with all colors in it and some very good not cheap, paint brushes.

This is a fun and rewarding hobby and will not cost you too much to start this project off. Anyway, lots of people like to paint because it is so relaxing.

In most communities around the country, even in small towns now are good and informative libraries. If you can still drive, this would be a relaxing and nice outing to go to, your local libraries, to check out

UNICORN HORSE. ANOTHER, WELL USED AFTER WARDS IS A MAGAZINE CONTAINER, SOME LOVELY PICTURE FRAMES ARE JUST DARLING OUT OF WOOD. WE PAINTED OURS WITH A LIGHT BLUE PAINT AND PAINTED SOME WHITE DAISIES ON THE FRONT OF THE FRAMES, VERY REFRESHING LOOK. AFTER, THIS YOU NEED TO GO OUT AND BUY SOME TWINE FOR THE BACK OF THESE PICTURE FRAMES, TO HANG THE FRAMES. TRY THIS PROJECT AS I THINK THAT YOU WILL REALLY LIKE THIS PROJECT. GOOD LUCK TO ALL OF YOU OUT THERE.

CHAPTER 6 SIX;

iT WOULD BE SIMPLE TO JUST SAY START IN YOUR KITCHEN COOKING BUT i AM QUIET SURE THAT SOMEWHERE ALONG THE LINE YOU HAVE COOKED A LOT IN YOUR OWN KITCHEN AT TIMES. TRY TO THINK ABOUT GOING OUT OF YOUR COMFORT ZONE AND SIGN UP FOR A COOKING COURSE OR A COOKING SCHOOL CLOSE BY YOU. IT WOULD DEFINETLY GET YOU OUT OF YOUR HOUSE AND GET YOU WITH OTHER PEOPLE YOU MIGHT ENJOY BEING AROUND. THIS IS A GOOD WAY TO SPEND YOUR DAYS WHEN YOU RETIRE. IT WILL GET YOU UP AND MOVING AND OUT OF THAT FAVORITE CHAIR OF YOURS WHERE YOU SIMPLY BECOME A COUCH POTATOE MOST OF YOUR TIME. THIS IS ALSO A WAY OF FINDING NEW THINGS TO LEARN HOW TO COOK AND STEAM. IF YOU HAVE OLD FAMILY RECEIPES TO SHARE WITH THE OTHER MEMBERS OF YOUR GROUP BY ALL MEANS DO SO. SOME FAVORITES WILL BE FROM YOUR MOTHER OR YOUR GRANDMOTHER OR YOUR AUNT'S OLD COOK BOOKS. EVEN I HAVE SOME VERY OLD FAVORITES I WOULD LIKE TO SHARE WITH YOU NOW.

RECEIPES: on the next pages.

Fast and easy chicken enchilada feast

Heirloom recipe handed down from: feast-chicken enchilada
Region of origin: Carribean   **Origin date: 1960**
Tradition: Breakfast or Dinner Bake **Prep time: 1hr   Servings: 6**

INGREDIENTS
8 ounces coarsely chopped chicken
1 can (4ounces) chilies drained and ???
chopped -2 green onions chop
½ cup mayonnaise
1 pressed garlic clove - chop fine
1 tablespoon of taco seasoning
3 tablespoon corn chips, chop and d???
cheese-4ozs.shredded-tortilla chip
broken up ⅓ bag. 2 packs of
Crescent rolls-one lime- Salsa or
sour cream. Heat oven 375-chop
ingredients, place on rollout dough

INSTRUCTIONS

Preheat oven to 375 degrees F.. Chop all engredients in a large bowl if not already chopped. Finely dice red pepper-green onion also. Add to bowl chicken and black olives diced-mayonnnaise. Next add grated cheese, pressed and diced garlic, corn, seasoning mix and any remaining ingredients. Next roll out the crescent rolls dough on a large about size of a cookie sheet (16 triangles) Arrange triangles in circle on baking tray wide ends overlapping in the center points outside. Now, fill with mixture to look like being stuffed on the widest end of rolled out dough. Bake until golden brown- place out of oven to cool add more chopped up corn tortilla chips from the bag. Cut lime into slices for a garnish. Serve while warm, with a sour creamcontainer, of sour cream or a soup bowl filled with salsa.

Homemade Baked Beans

Bring a pan of baked beans to any gathering, and everyone will have a scoop of their favorite side.

By Southern Living Test Kitchen | Updated on April 21, 2023

Active Time: 15 mins
Bake Time: 45 mins
Total Time: 1 hrs

Ingredients

Cooking spray
4 bacon slices
1 small onion, diced
4 (15-ounce) cans pork and beans in tomato sauce, drain
½ cup ketchup
1 ½ teaspoons Worcestershire sauce
⅓ cup firmly packed brown sugar
1 teaspoon dry mustard
½ cup sorghum syrup or molasses

Directions

Step 1
Cook bacon and onions:

Preheat oven to 350 F. Grease an 11- x 7-inch baking dish with cooking spray.

Cook bacon in a skillet over medium-high heat 4 minutes; drain, reserving 1 teaspoon drippings in skillet.

Step 2
Saute onion in hot bacon drippings 7 minutes or until tender.

Stir together pork, onions, beans, and next 5 ingredients in a lightly greased 11- x 7-inch baking dish. Top bean mixture with bacon.

Step 3
Bake at 350 F for 45 minutes or until bubbly.

Additional reporting by **Alexandra Emanuelli**

♥ **RECIPE**

Carrot Cake Cheesecake Cake

★ ★ ★ ★ ★ 5 from 2 reviews

Author: **Lindsay** *Prep Time:* **1 hour 20 minutes** *Chill Time:* **4 hours**
Cook Time: **2 hours 10 minutes** *Total Time:* **7 hours 30 minutes** *Yield:*
14-16 slices *Category:* **Dessert** *Method:* **Oven** *Cuisine:* **American**

Ingredients

CINNAMON CHEESECAKE

24 oz (678g) cream cheese, room temperature
1 cup (207g) sugar
3 tbsp (24g) all purpose flour
½ cup (115g) sour cream
1 tbsp vanilla extract
2 tsp ground cinnamon
3 large eggs, room temperature

CARROT CAKE

two 9 inch cake layers of Carrot Cake

CREAM CHEESE FROSTING

16 oz (452g) cream cheese, room temperature
¾ cup (172g) butter, room temperature
10 cups (1150g) powdered sugar
2 tsp vanilla extract
2 ½ cups (275g) chopped pecans

Instructions

Blueberry Compote Instructions

1. Combine frozen blueberries, sugar and cornstarch in medium saucepan and bring to a boil over medium-high heat, stirring frequently. Reduce heat and simmer 5 minutes, stirring occasionally.

2. Remove from heat and cool to room temperature. Refrigerate until mixture is a thick jam-like consistency, at least 8 hours.

PULL APART BREAD INSTRUCTIONS

1. Preheat oven to 375 F. Generously grease a 9-inch x 5-inch loaf pan with nonstick cooking spray or butter.

2. Divide each piece of biscuit dough into thirds. Spoon 1 teaspoon chilled blueberry compote into the center of one dough piece. Carefully fold dough over top of the blueberry compote and firmly pinch the seams closed. If necessary, wet edges of dough with cold water to secure seams. Roll filled dough gently between your hands to smooth out the seams and form a ball. Repeat until all pieces of dough are filled. (You will have additional blueberry compote left to serve with baked pull apart bread.)

3. Microwave butter in a bowl until melted.

4. Combine sugar and cinnamon in another bowl.

5. Dip each stuffed dough ball in melted butter, then roll in cinnamon sugar and arrange in prepared loaf pan, forming two layers.

6. Bake 30-35 minutes or until top of loaf is golden brown, has puffed up and is baked through.

7. Let stand for 10 minutes.

8. Serve hot with remaining blueberry compote.

About This Recipe

Instructions

TO MAKE THE CHEESECAKE:

1. Preheat oven to 300 F (148 C). Line the entire inside of a 9 inch cake pan with aluminum foil. Press it into the pan to get it as flat as you can. You'll use the aluminum foil to lift the cheesecake out of the pan when it's baked and cooled.

2. In a large mixer bowl, mix the cream cheese, sugar and flour together until combined. Use low speed to keep less air from getting into the batter, which can cause cracks. Scrape down the sides of the bowl.

3. Add the sour cream, vanilla extract and and cinnamon and mix on low speed until well combined.

4. Add the eggs one at a time, mixing slowly and scraping the sides of the bowl after each addition.

5. Pour the cheesecake batter into the lined cake pan.

6. Place the cake pan inside another larger pan. I use a larger cake pan, but you can use a roasting pan or any other larger baking pan. Fill the outside pan with enough warm water to go about halfway up the sides of the cake pan. Bake for 45 minutes.

7. Turn off the oven and leave the cheesecake in the oven with the door closed for 30 minutes. Do not open the door or you'll release the heat.

8. Crack oven door and leave the cheesecake in the oven for another 30 minutes. This cooling process helps the cheesecake cool slowly to prevent cracks.

9. Remove cheesecake from oven and chill until firm, 4-5 hours.

TO MAKE THE CARROT CAKE LAYERS:

1. Make my carrot cake, but bake in two 9 inch cake pans (I recommend using the same pan as you did for the cheesecake so

they are the same size) for 32-36 minutes, or until a toothpick inserted comes out with just a few moist crumbs.

TO MAKE THE FROSTING AND ASSEMBLE THE CAKE:

1. To make the frosting, add the cream cheese and butter to a large mixer bowl and beat until well combined and smooth.

2. Add about half of the powdered sugar and mix until well combined and smooth.

3. Add the vanilla extract and mix until well combined.

4. Add the remaining powdered sugar and mix until well combined and smooth. Add more or less powdered sugar, as desired for consistency purposes.

5. Use a large serrated knife to remove the domes from the top of the two carrot cakes, if needed.

6. Place the first layer of cake on a serving plate or a cardboard cake round. Spread about 1 cup of frosting evenly on top of the cake layer.

7. Use the aluminum foil to lift the cheesecake out of the cake pan, remove the foil and place the cheesecake on top of the cake. The cheesecake should be firm and solid and easy to move around.

8. Spread another cup of frosting evenly on top of the cheesecake, then add the second layer of cake on top. If the sides of the cake don't line up, use a serrated knife to trim off the excess cake or cheesecake.

9. Frost the outside of the cake, then press the pecans into the sides of the cake.

10. Pipe shells of the frosting around the top edge of the cake. I used the Ateco 847 icing tip. Finish off the cake with some additional chopped pecans.

11. Store the cake (in an airtight container, if possible) in the refrigerator until ready to serve. This cake is full of moisture and lasts very well. Best if eaten with 4-5 days.

Nutrition

Serving Size: 1 Slice   **Calories:** 853   **Sugar:** 50.4 g   **Sodium:** 505.9 mg   **Fat:** 56.4 g

Carbohydrates: 75.7 g   **Protein:** 15.3 g   **Cholesterol:** 198 mg

Find it online: *https//www.lifeloveandsugar.com/carrot-cake-cheesecake-cake/*

A RAPTIVE PARTNER SITE

No-Bake Cheesecake

This easy, classic dessert is just right for any occasion.

By Martha Stewart Test Kitchen   Updated on April 24, 2023

Prep Time: 25 mins
Total Time: 3 hrs 30 mins

Ingredients

2 packages (20 sheets) graham crackers
11 tablespoons (1 ⅜ sticks) unsalted butter, melted
2 tablespoons sugar
2 8-ounce packages cream cheese, room temperature
1 14-ounce can (1 ¼ cups) sweetened condensed milk
¼ cup fresh lemon juice
1 teaspoon vanilla extract

Directions

Step 1
Crush graham crackers:

Put graham crackers in a large resealable plastic bag, and crush them with a rolling pin until very fine crumbs form.

Step 2
Mix graham-cracker crumbs with sugar and butter:

Pour crumbs into a medium bowl; stir in sugar. Add butter and stir until well combined.

Step 3
Press crumb mixture into springform pan:

Press the crumb mixture into a 9-inch springform pan, spreading it 1 ½ to 2 inches up the side; press flat. Chill crust in freezer at least 10 minutes.

Broccoli Quiche Bites - (Snacks for parties.)

After the pastry thaws, it takes just 10 minutes to put together these easy-to-make appetizers that get lots of flavor from a surprising ingredient - vegetable soup mix.

Ingredients

0.5 of a 17.3-ounce package Pepperidge Farm® Puff Pastry Sheets (1 sheet), thawed
4 egg beaten
1 envelope dry vegetable soup and dip mix
1 package (10 ounces) chopped frozen broccoli cuts, thawed and well drained
1 cup whipped cottage cheese
0.5 cup shredded Cheddar cheese (about 2 ounces)

Heat the oven to 375 F. Lightly grease a 9x13-inch shallow baking dish.

Stir the eggs, soup mix, broccoli and cottage cheese in a medium bowl. Cover and refrigerate for 20 minutes.

Unfold the pastry sheet on a lightly floured surface. Roll the pastry sheet into a 9x13-inch rectangle. Place the pastry into the bottom of the baking dish. Prick the pastry with a fork.

Spread the broccoli mixture in the baking dish. Sprinkle with the Cheddar cheese.

Bake for 30 minutes or until set. Let stand in the baking dish on a wire rack for 20 minutes. Cut into 24 pieces.

Homemade Deep Dish Pizza with Sausage & Peppers

Skip some steps in this meaty deep dish pizza by using refrigerated dough, cooked pepperoni and smoked sausage and a frozen veggie blend. Simply layer the ingredients, pour on the ??? soup, sprinkle with oregano and bake up some deliciousness.

Ingredients

1 tablespoon olive oil

1 package (13.8 ounces) refrigerated pizza crush dough

0.5 cup sliced pepperoni

7 ounces smoked pork sausage, diced (about 1 ½ cups)

1 cup frozen pepper and onion blend, thawed, drained and patted dry

1 package (8 ounces) shredded pizza cheese blend (about 2 cups)

1 can (10 ¾ ounces) Campbell's® Condensed Tomato Soup

1 teaspoon dried oregano leaves, crushed

Heat the oven to 450 F. Brush the oil on the inside of a 9-inch round cake pan. Roll the dough into ???-inch square. Press the dough into the bottom and up the sides of the cake pan, letting the excess dough drape over the edge of the pan.

Layer the dough with the pepperoni sausage and pepper and onion blend. Top with half the cheese. Spread the soup over the cheese. Sprinkle one oregano. Top with the remaining cheese. Fold the excess dough bark into the pan over the cheese.

Bake for 30 minutes or until deep golden brown (if the crust is getting too dark cover the pizza loosely with foil). Let the pizza cool in the pan for 15 minutes. Using a spatula (careful- the pan will still be hot) remove the pizza to a cutting board. Cut and serve.

Deviled Egg Macaroni Pasta Salad

All the deliciousness of deviled eggs and pasta salad in one colorful side dish! This macaroni pasta salad is perfect for family gatherings and is kid friendly. One serving is never enough!

By BHG Test Kitchen   Updated on August 4, 2022

Prep Time: 30 mins
Total Time: 30 mins

Ingredients

½ cup thinly sliced red onion

¼ cup cider vinegar

1 teaspoon sugar

8 ounce large elbow macaroni

12 hard-cooked eggs

½ cup mayonnaise

3 tablespoon country Dijon-style mustard

½ teaspoon salt

½ teaspoon smoked paprika

¼ teaspoon cracked black pepper

½ cup chopped sweet pickle

1 ½ cup very thinly sliced celery

Smoked paprika and/or pepper (optional)

Directions

Step 1
In a small saucepan combine onion, vinegar and sugar. Bring to a simmer, stirring occasionally. Remove from heat; set aside.

Step 2
Meanwhile, cook macaroni according to package directions. Drain and rinse well with cold water; set aside.

Step 3
Coarsely chop one egg; set aside. Halve remaining eggs; separate yolks from whites. Coarsely chop egg whites; set aside.

Step 4
For dressing, place yolks in a medium bowl; mash with a fork. Add mayonnaise, mustard, and onion and vinegar mixture. Gradually stir in 2 Tbsp. water, salt, paprika, and pepper. Set aside.

Step 5

In a large bowl combine the egg whites, pickles, celery, macaroni, and dressing; toss to combine. Top with reserved egg; sprinkle with additional smoked paprika and pepper. Serve at once or cover and chill up to 6 hours. If the mixture gets a little dry after storing, you can stir in a little milk.

Nutrition Facts

Per serving: 273 calories; total fat 15g; saturated fat 3g; cholesterol 228mg; sodium 422mg; total carbohydrate 21g; total sugars 4; protein 11g; vitamin c 1.2mg; calcium 50mg; iron 1.6mg; potassium 195mg; folate, total 87.9mcg; vitamin b-12 0.7mcg; vitamin b-6 0.1mg

New Orleans-Style Pralines

Submitted by PanNan

"This is Brennan's recipe. They keep them by the front door for patrons to enjoy. So creamy, nutty and delicious! Note - these melt in your mouth, they are not the chewy kind."

??? Ready In: 30 mins

??? Ingredients: 5

??? Yields: 3 trays

??? Serves: 30

DIRECTIONS

1. Line 3 baking sheets with parchment paper (important to have these ready because you'll have to work fast when they're done).

2. In a large saucepan, simmer cream, sugar, corn syrup and orange zest slowly over low heat, until reduced (watch carefully for boil over).

3. Stir continuously as soon as the mixture starts to stick to the bottom of the pan (the mixture will become thicker and turn light brown as is reduces and the sugar carmelizes).

4. Stir in pecans when the mixture reaches the soft-ball stage (240 degrees), and continue to stir until the mixture starts to pull away from the sides of the pan.

5. Test by dropping a quarter size amount onto the lined baking sheet, and if it holds a nice rounded top (instead of running out flat), and if it is dull looking (rather than oily/shiny) it is ready (approximately 248 degrees).

6. Use two dessert spoons to spoon out the pralines onto the baking sheets (one to dip, and one to scrape off) - they're hot, be careful!

7. Depending on the humidity, temperature, and luck - they may be ready in about 30 minutes, but don't worry - it could take up to a day or two.

8. Store in an airtight container up to a week.

♥ RECIPE

Moist Vanilla Layer Cake

★ ★ ★ ★ ★ **4.9 from 111 reviews**

Author: **Life, Love and Sugar** *Prep Time:* **1 hour 20 minutes** *Cook Time:* **25 minutes** *Total Time:* **1 hour 45 minutes** *Yield:* **12-14 Slices** *Category:* **Dessert** *Method:* **Oven** *Cuisine:* **American**

Description

Everyone needs to know how to make this moist vanilla layer cake. Three layers of moist, fluffy vanilla cake are filled and frosted with rich vanilla buttercream. It's absolutely heavenly.

Ingredients

VANILLA CAKE

2 ½ cups (325g) all purpose flour
2 ½ tsp baking powder
½ tsp salt

¾ cup (168g) unsalted butter, room temperature

¼ cup vegetable oil

1 ½ cups (310g) sugar

1 tbsp vanilla extract

4 large eggs

1 ¼ cups (300ml) milk

VANILLA FROSTING

3 cups (672g) unsalted butter, room temperature

12 cups (1380g) powdered sugar

1 tbsp vanilla extract

6–7 tbsp (90-105ml) water or milk

Salt, to taste

Violet gel icing color

Cornflower blue gel icing color

Sprinkles*

Instructions

FOR THE CAKE:

1. Prepare three 8 inch cake pans with parchment paper circles in the bottom and grease the sides. Preheat oven to 350 F (176 C).

2. Combine the flour, baking powder and salt in a medium sized bowl and set aside.

3. Add the butter, sugar, oil and vanilla extract to a large mixer bowl and beat together until light in color and fluffy, about 2-3 minutes. Do not skimp on the creaming time.

4. Add the eggs one at a time, mixing until mostly combined after each. Scrape down the sides of the bowl as needed to be sure all ingredients are well incorporated.

5. Add half of the dry ingredients to the batter and mix until mostly combined.

6. Slowly add the milk and mix until well combined. The batter will look curdled, but that's ok.

7. Add the remaining dry ingredients and mix until well combined and smooth. Scrape down the sides of the bowl as needed to be sure all ingredients are well incorporated. Do not over mix the batter.

8. Divide the batter evenly between the cakes pans and bake for 22-25 minutes, or until a toothpick comes out with a few crumbs.

9. Remove the cakes from the oven and allow to cool for about 2-3 minutes, then remove to cooling racks to cool completely.

FOR THE FROSTING:

1. To make the frosting, beat the butter until smooth.

2. Slowly add half of the powdered sugar and mix until smooth.

3. Add the vanilla extract, 4-5 tablespoons of water or milk and salt and mix until smooth.

4. Slowly add the remaining powdered sugar and mix until smooth. Add additional water or milk, as needed to get the right consistency of frosting.

TO ASSEMBLE THE CAKE:

1. To put the cake together, use a large serrated knife to remove the domes from the top of the cakes so that they're flat. These cakes don't have a large dome, but I like to make sure they're completely flat.

2. Place the first cake on a serving plate or a cardboard cake round.

3. Spread about 1 cup of frosting evenly on top of the cake.

4. Add the second layer of cake and another cup of frosting.

5. Top the cake with the remaining layer and frost the outside of the cake. Refer to my tutorial for frosting a smooth cake, if needed.

6. Press sprinkles into the sides of the cake.

7. Color the remaining frosting to your desired shade. I used a mix of purple and cornflower blue gel icing color.

8. Pipe swirls of frosting around the top edge of the cake. I used Ateco tip 844.

9. Add a few more sprinkles to the top of the cake. Store in an air-tight container. Cake is best for 3-4 days.

I used a mix of sprinkles similar to this Sweetapolitas sprinkle medley and ones similar to these rainbow sprinkles.

Notes

1. For cupcakes, use the same temperature. Fill cupcake liners 3/4 full and bake for 13-15 minutes or until a toothpick inserted in the middle comes out with a few crumbs. This recipe should make about 24-28 cupcakes.

Nutrition

Serving Size: 1 slice	Calories: 1032	Sugar: 106.7 g	Sodium: 192.4 mg
Fat: 57.4 g	Carbohydrates: 126.2 g	Protein: 6.8 g	Cholesterol: 135.1 mg

Find it online: https://www.lifeloveandsugar.com/moist-vanilla-layer-cake/

––––––––––––––––––––––––

A RAPTIVE PARTNER SITE

Baked Beans from Scratch

These baked beans from scratch are made by combining navy beans, molasses, and maple syrup to make this classic dish at home.

Recipe by wkndyummychef Updated on July 22, 2022

Prep Time: 10 mins
Cook Time: 7 hrs 20 mins
Total Time: 7 hrs 30 mins

Ingredients

1 cup navy beans, soaked overnight and drained
4 cups water
¼ cup ketchup
¼ cup maple syrup
2 tablespoons brown sugar
2 tablespoons molasses
1 teaspoon Worcestershire sauce
½ teaspoon salt
⅛ teaspoon ground black pepper

⅛ teaspoon chili powder
1 small onion, chopped

Directions

Step 1
Place beans in a large saucepan with 4 cups of water. Bring to a boil over high heat, then reduce heat to medium-low, cover, and simmer 1 hour.

Step 2
Preheat the oven to 375 degrees F (190 degrees C). Stir ketchup, maple syrup, brown sugar, molasses, Worcestershire sauce, salt, pepper, and chili powder together in a small bowl; set aside.

Step 3
Once beans have simmered for 1 hour, drain, and reserve cooking liquid. Pour beans into a 1 1/2-quart casserole dish; stir in chopped onion and molasses mixture. Stir in enough reserved cooking liquid so sauce covers beans by 1/4 inch.

Step 4

Cover and bake in the preheated oven for 10 minutes; reduce heat to 200 degrees F (95 degrees C) and cook 6 hours longer, stirring beans after they have cooked for 3 hours. Once beans are tender and sauce has reduced and is sticky, remove from the oven, stir, recover, and allow to stand 15 minutes before serving.

Quick-Soak Option:

Place navy beans into a large pot and cover with several inches of cold water; bring to a boil over high heat. Once boiling, turn off the heat, cover, and let stand 1 hour. Drain and rinse before using.

Nutrition Facts

Per serving: 122 calories; total fat 0g; sodium 196mg; total carbohydrate 26g; dietary fiber 5g; total sugars 12g; protein 5g; vitamin c 2mg; calcium 53mg; iron 2mg; potassium 364mg

Skillet Salsa Shrimp With Spinach and Feta

A quick and easy seafood delight.

BY THE PREVENTION TEST KITCHEN   PUBLISHED: JAN 27, 2022

YIELDS:

4

TOTAL TIME:

15 mins

Ingredients   ??? SAVE RECIPE

1 tbsp. olive oil

4 cloves garlic, finely chopped

3 strips lemon zest, thinly sliced

½ 15.5 oz. jar salsa

8 oz. tomato sauce

20 shrimp, peeled and deveined

2 c. baby spinach

¼ c. crumbled feta, for serving

Flatbread, for serving

Directions

Step 1
Heat olive oil, garlic, and lemon zest in a large skillet on medium until beginning to brown, about 1 min.

Step 2
Add salsa and tomato sauce and bring to a simmer. Nestle shrimp in the salsa mixture and cook, covered, 3 min.

Step 3
Fold in spinach and cook until beginning to wilt and shrimp are opaque throughout, 1 to 2 min. more.

Step 4
Sprinkle with feta and serve with flatbread if desired.

Nutrition per serving: 121 cal, 8 g pro, 9 g carb, 3 g fiber, 4.5 sugars (0 g added sugars), 6 g fat (2 g sat fat), 52 mg chol, 966 mg sodium

Unknown to the public there are several reasons why certain states refuse to set up Gambling Cascinos in their states but if you are terribly bored to death you can take a nice trip to a state close by you and have yourself a good vacation near to a gaming cacino. This is a real break whenever you can play a fun slot machine. ONCE, you go over to play try and stay a night or two in their hotel and have yourself some wonderful food at their buffet or oyster bar or just a snack at their ice cream and yougart palor. Some of the larger cascinos have lovely gift shops that you can spend at least an hour in looking at all of the nice gifts that they have to offer in them.

Often, in a few of the larger ones they do have free drinks and come around with a food cart. You, may have to play $5.00 first before you do get a mixed drink or beer. Please, call ahead if you would like to reserve a room at their hotel. We usually stay one or two nights so we can look around the area.

college days

if you are close to the south try to go to visit in Louisiana because the fishing is so good over there and also the shrimping is even better in Louisiana. In Florida you have the bigger fish, the game fish, tarpon, large red fish, sharks, some type of octopus, white fish.

Over and over are the tourists who love the fishing in Florida. Destin, Florida has some wonderful tour boats who take you out for a price and charter boats, with rods and reels and also bait for a reasonable price. These are happy times and so lovely out on the Gulf of Mexico, right at dusk.

I know that most of us would just love to have a nice beach right around us but the truth of this is most of that property is already sold for a outrageous price and most of the reasonable lots for sale have gone up in price tremendously in the past five years. If you manage to get to some of the beaches around the Gulf of Mexico, near the coast you are very lucky people indeed. These beaches hold so much beauty and the water is very safe to swimm in. Lots of beaches you have to pay just to sit on a blanket to enjoy yourself are up North, like New Jersey. Florida, are the best of the best beaches, with crystal clear water and clean white sand. Mississippi, Gulf coast beaches are also very nice too. A lot of people like the South Carolina and the Virginia coast line, which is so very lovely in the nicer spring and summer months. If you love to do alot of fishing then Louisiana is the right place for you. They have out standing fishing and shrimping areas in that state.

Chapter 7

Everyone of us seems to have a favorite habit but when you get older, THERE COMES A TIME WHEN YOU REALIZE THAT YOU CAN NOT DO AS MUCH AS YOU WOULD LIKE TOO. A TOTAL AND COMPLETE TIME WHEN YOU FEEL ALONE AND LONELY. THIS IS TO ENSURE THAT YOUR TIME WILL BE SOMEWHAT OF A PLEASURE FOR YOU BY LOOKING INTO ADOPTING OR BUYING YOURSELF A PET OF SOME TYPE, A DOG OR A CUDDLEY KITTEN, A FISH TANK WHERE YOU CAN WATCH THE FISH FOR AN HOUR OR TWO. KEEP IN MIND THAT SOME ANIMALS ARE VERY KNOWN TO BE SMART AND DO WATCH OVER YOU IF YOU FALL, GET CAUGHT IN A BAD RAIN STORM, LOOSE YOUR WAY HOME, ETC. ANIMALS, ESPECIALLY DOGS OF ALL KINDS ARE LIKE HAVING A PERSON AROUND TO KEEP YOU COMPANY. ONCE WE HAD TWO PETS WHO TOOK LONG WALKS WITH US AND IF YOU TOLD THEM TO GO AND DO SOMETHING THEY WENT RIGHT AWAY AND DID IT. SOME TIME THEY WOULD LOOK LIKE THEY UNDERSTOOD EVERY SINGLE WORD THAT YOU SAID,

TO THEM. NOW, IF YOU CAN AFFORD A PET, BELIEVE ME IT WOULD HELP YOUR BOREDOM AND YOUR PEACE OF MIND IN YOUR OLD AGE. ALSO GIVE YOUR SPIRITS A TOTAL LIFT TOO. PICKING OUT A NAME FOR YOUR NEW PET IS A LOT OF FUN AND YOU CAN GET OTHERS IN YOUR FAMILY TO HELP WITH THE NEW NAME FOR YOUR NEW PET. WE HAD A WONDERFUL PUPPY NAMED PEACHES. SHE WAS SUCH A LOVE AND LIVED A VERY LONG LIFE ALL THE WAY UNTIL HER DEATH AT 17 VERY HAPPY YEARS. ALSO RIGHT AFTER PEACHES PASSED WE HAD A LARGE BLACK AND WHITE CAT NAMED HOOKIE THREE WHO LOVED HER NEW PLAYMATE, OUR NEW OLDER DOG NAMED CINNAMON. THE TWO OF THEM WERE SUCH FRIENDS THAT CINNAMON WOULD ACTUALLY LOOK FOR OUR CAT IN THE MORNING WHEN SHE GOT UP AND KISS HOOKIE, RIGHT ON HER MOUTH. IT WAS SO FUNNY TO WATCH THIS EVERY DAY. THE TWO OF THEM WERE CLOSE AND WATCHED OUT FOR ONE ANOTHER ALWAYS. BOTH OF THEM LIVED A VERY LONG LIFE. SOME TIMES YOU CAN GET A SHELTER DOG FOR FREE AT THE ANIMAL RESCUE CENTER AROUND YOUR AREA, WHERE YOU LIVE

OR THE NEAR BY LARGER TOWN. YOU, CAN CHECK THIS OUT OVER THE INTERNET BY GOING TO THE SEARCH BAR ON YOUR COMPUTER OR JUST CALLING YOUR LOCAL ANIMAL SHELTER. DON'T FORGET IF YOU CAN AFFORD A NICE PET THEY ARE SURELY A BLESSING.

Chapter 5

SAKI Large Porcelain Te???
48 Ounce Tea Pot with I???
Loose Leaf and Bloomin???
Pot - Red

Color: Red

Note: The following pages are suggestions <u>only</u> and may not be for sake; when this book is published.

plans on this enterprise and said no more of this. Still and all we learned a lot and still use this knowledge today. No one ever really knows what is the best after retirement jobs to stay busy because things change so very fast in this world just like the stock market does change so quickly as it always seems too.

A Fun Chapter

in this last section of my retirement book, i chose two of the most famous cities to visit and to take their tours as these are some of the most famous places i could think of to visit and there are lots and lots of interesting things to do. The cities are new Orleans, louisiana and Nashville, Tennessee. Most require you to call and make your plans early and see if you will fit in on the dates that you would like to tour the different attractions there.

one might take along their water bottle, a sun hat in the summer months while there and also some sun screen. it depends also on the time of the day you plan to be out and about in these cities. TAKE, comfortable shoes and if you like a back pack with a few energy snacks too. You, will be delighted at the different things their are to do while there. I USUALLY, take a small purse for extra coupons and money. Sometimes just a money belt with enough room for eye drops and meds. and cleanex. GO, for it and just have yourselves a very fun time, laugh a lot as it always helps me to break any tension that I am experiencing at the time.

Belle Meade Guided Mansion Tour with ...

Love this!

Ryman Auditorium "Mother Church of Country ...

Discover Nashville City Tour with Entry to Ryman ...

Musicians Hall of Fame and Museum Admission ...

Ryman Auditorium "Mother Church of Country ...

2 hr - Historic Downtown Nashville to ...

Grand Ole Opry House Guided Backstage Tour

Belle Meade Guided Mansion Tour with ...

One of the most famous and popular parks in Nashville, Centennial Park is located on 32 acres of land, and is filled with a plethora of entertaining activities and beauty for its visitors to enjoy. This park is visited by tens of thousands of people every year due its impressive statutes, museum and festivals. Centennial Park received its name for being the site of the Tennessee Centennial Exposition. A ...

Experience the taste of Nashville with Nashville Hop On Hop Off Trolley Tour () - a culinary angle to Centennial Park.

Nashville Hop On Hop Off Trolley Tour

RYMAN AUDITORIUM

Ryman Auditorium, included in the National Register of Historic Places in 1971, is a massive live performance venue with over 2,300 seats for guests. From 1943 until 1974 it hosted the Grand Ole Opry's weekly performances and became a national icon. Sponsored by a wealthy Nashville Business man, Thomas Ryman, the Union Gospel Tabernacle was built in 1892 as a tabernacle for Samuel Porter Jones, an ...

Save valuable time and money by getting Ryman Auditorium tickets () in advance.

Ryman Auditorium "Mother Church of Country Music" Self-Guided Tour

2 hr - Historic Downtown Nashville to ...

CENTENNIAL PARK

Belle Meade Guided Mansion Tour with ...

Belmont Mansion All Day Admission Ticket in ...

Welcome to Nashville: Private Tour with Johnny ...

Discover Nashville City Tour with Entry to Ryman ...

chapter nine 9 - college days

This is another chapter on my manuscript that i think most of you all will enjoy. since my precious family could not afford to send me to college when i did graduate from high school somehow i knew, that some day i would have the chanch to get to go to a college but i did not know that it would be when i was a senior and 62 years of age.

long, long time. All of the colleges were so expensive that this had been only a dream of mine, for a very long time. One day a young girl i had never met before started telling me about the college that she was attending was paying for her to take five courses at a junior college and our government was somehow pitching in to pay for all of this. I inquired later on and did find out if you had never been to college before and you had reached a certain age you could attend classes that you wished to take and not come up with hardly any money at all. Right away i signed up for all of this and became seems like over night a college student at a junior college. THE FIRST WEEK, I was very nervous but once i settled down and took the SAT's. after that everything seemed to fall into place. The college professors seemed to like me and did suggest that i invite my husband to sign up for college courses too. He eventually did and just loved it. Every morning we would leave our house, take our coffee in insulated coffee mug and get to college in plenty of time to talk with the other students there. ALL of our fellow students seemed schocked to see us old folks there with them every single morning. Each and every one of them seemed to be so very respectful towards us and they seemed to be so happy to see us each and every day in class. Always we came home that evening and completed out home work assignments. All, of our teachers liked us giving the others examples of how we had lived our lives and what jobs we had taken in our life times. To tell you the truth i just liked getting up in the mornings having something to look forward too and my husband did too. we seemed to be getting along those days much better than just sitting in our living room watching the tube and programs on the television set. GOD, had surely shined on us and when the year was up we received very excellent grades in each subject we had taken. We still have some laughs over everything that went on in class. The hurricane hit our communities that year and it took alot of work in the computer classes to get finished with all of work we wanted to accomplish. Try this out and i am very sure that you will definitely get a lot out of it and make many new friends also. It is a wise idea and you will find out that it is not very hard on your budget at all.

THESE ARE ITEMS YOU MIGHT WANT TO HAVE ON SUCCEEDING IN YOUR COLLEGE COURSES:

1. *A LARGE AND WELL MADE FOUNTAIN PEN.*
2. *A BACK SACK FOR YOUR COURSE BOOKS.*
3. *LOTS OF COMPUTER PAPER (WHITE & BLANK).*
4. *EXTRA PADS TO WRITE HOMEWORK ASSIGNMENTS ON.*
5. *BOOKS THAT THE PROFESSERS TELL YOU THAT YOU NEED TO SECURE BEFORE YOU BEGIN CLASSES.*
6. *COFFEE OR Water container for drinking when tirstey.*
7. *Dictionary for Spelling and for meaning of certain words.*
8. *Bottle of white out (ink eraser).*
9. *Healthy snacks if you get very hungrey before next class.*

Chapter 11

These can definetly be some of the best years of your life if you can just stay focused and have something to look forward to when you do get up every morning. All of us have something we do enjoy whether it be cooking, fishing, playing golf, swimming, woodworking, sewing, knitting, or simply playing around on your computer.

One day you simply need to take the time to check out some of the gyms close to your house. a large gym is more fun than a smaller one because more people will exercise and getting into shape at any age that you are. A larger gym will have more people you can make friends with. They too are taking the time to stay fit. Some towns have a YMCA with a nice gym with lots of machines too exercise in. One other point is that some of these particular places have nice swimming in door pools that can certainly be enjoyed any time of the day when you get there, unless the pool is being cleaned on that day. Lots of families like to go in the evening so they can sign up some other family members. Most insurance companies are now paying the gyms by the month to keep seniors active and staying healthy.

Do try this and do enjoy your new freedom to get out of your house and off of your favorite chair or sofa. This will be the best years of your retirement is now so just take some time to act on some of these suggestions i have given to you in my book and go for it. Good luck to you and God bless you.

<u>The End</u>

Printed in the United States
by Baker & Taylor Publisher Services